Fresh Farm Facts

- Hens will usually lay 260 eggs per year! 
- Potatoes can grow from a whole potato or a piece that has an "eye!" 
- There are more than 15 types of tomatoes, like Big Beef, Rose, and Jet Star!  
- Muzzle, withers, gaskin and flank are parts of a horse.
- Dutch, Mini Lop and Netherland Dwarf are three types of rabbits.
- Lettuce is part of the sunflower family!
- A cow can produce 46,000 glasses of milk a year!
- Many carrots are orange but can be purple, red and white! 
- One pound of wool can make 10 miles of yarn!
- A fresh egg yolk stands up and an old egg yolk flattens.

1

TURBINE
A TALL OBJECT THAT USES WIND TO CREATE POWER

BARN
A FARM BUILDING USED FOR STORAGE AND WORKSPACE THAT CAN ALSO HOUSE ANIMALS

PASTURE
A FIELD WHERE COWS OR HORSES GRAZE ON GRASS

CHICKEN COOP
A BUILDING WHERE CHICKENS ARE KEPT. THEY LAY EGGS IN A "NEST BOX"

KICKFLITTER FARMS

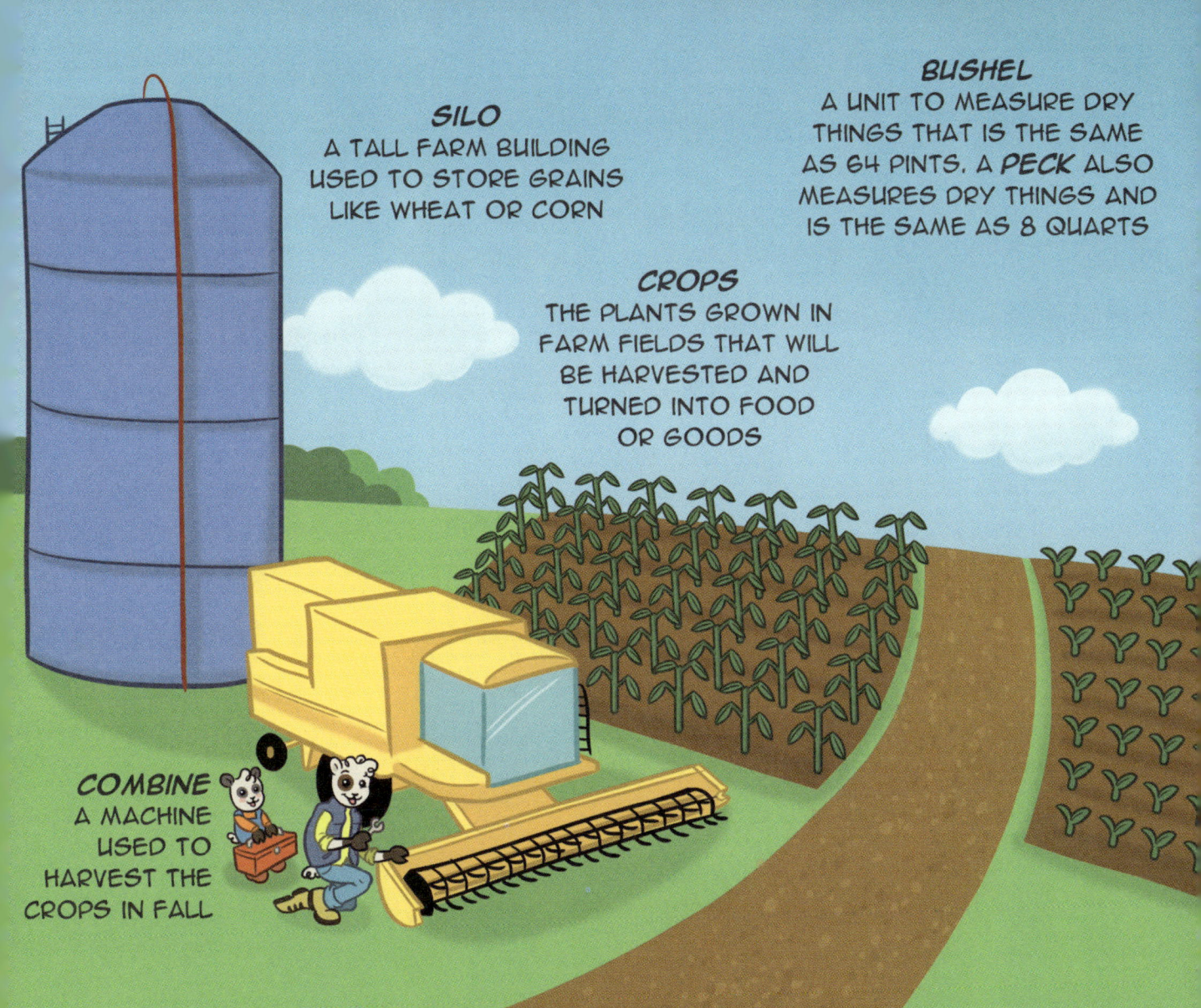

SILO
A TALL FARM BUILDING USED TO STORE GRAINS LIKE WHEAT OR CORN

BUSHEL
A UNIT TO MEASURE DRY THINGS THAT IS THE SAME AS 64 PINTS. A **PECK** ALSO MEASURES DRY THINGS AND IS THE SAME AS 8 QUARTS

CROPS
THE PLANTS GROWN IN FARM FIELDS THAT WILL BE HARVESTED AND TURNED INTO FOOD OR GOODS

COMBINE
A MACHINE USED TO HARVEST THE CROPS IN FALL

IT WAS A FARM FRESH SATURDAY AT KICKFLITTER FARMS. THE JONES FAMILY WAS BUSY WITH THEIR BUSHELS, PECKS, AND CHECKLISTS OF CHORES. IT TOOK A LOT TO KEEP THE FARM RUNNING, BUT THEY LOVED EVERY BIT OF IT! THAT AFTERNOON, THUMBS UP JOHNNIE CAME BY TO DROP OFF SOME HONEY FROM HIS VERY OWN BEES AND TO SEE IF HE COULD LEND A HELPING HAND.

HORSING AROUND
INSIDE THE
BARN!

TRACTOR
A SLOW, STRONG VEHICLE USED TO PULL THINGS

THUMBS UP JOHNNIE FOLLOWED FARMER ELI JONES INTO THE BARN WHERE HE WOULD HELP FEED THE HORSES AND PUT OIL INTO THE TRACTOR. BOTH INSIDE AND OUT, THERE WERE MANY THINGS TO DO TO KEEP THE FARM IN SILO-TOP SHAPE!

4

LOFT
THE UPPER AREA IN A BARN USED TO STORE HAY AND OTHER ITEMS

STALL
AN ENCLOSED AREA WHERE A HORSE OR OTHER ANIMAL STAYS

HAY
A DRIED AND CUT GRASS USED TO FEED ANIMALS

BARREL
A ROUND WOODEN CONTAINER USED TO STORE LIQUIDS

5

CORN
A GRAIN USED FOR FOOD LIKE CORN ON THE COB

HAY
A GRASS USED TO FEED ANIMALS LIKE COWS

SOYBEANS
A BEAN USED TO MAKE MANY THINGS LIKE CRAYONS

HECTARE
A UNIT THAT MEASURES AN AREA THAT IS 10,000 SQUARE METERS OR 2.47 ACRES

6

THUMBS UP JOHNNIE JOINED THE JONES FAMILY OUT IN THE FIELDS TO CHECK ON ALL THEIR CROPS. BUTTON WAS EXCITED TO RIDE IN THE COMBINE WITH HIS MOM, OLLIE, WHILE EWELA AND ELI MADE SURE THE CROPS WERE FERTILIZED. EVERYTHING WAS GROWING HEALTHY AND HEARTY AND WOULD SOON BE READY FOR HARVEST!

"A SCARECROW IS MADE OUT OF OLD CLOTHES AND USED IN FIELDS TO SCARE AWAY BIRDS."

COTTON
A FIBER USED TO MAKE CLOTHES AND YARN

WHEAT
A GRAIN USED TO MAKE FOODS LIKE BREAD AND CAKE

SORGHUM
A GRAIN USED TO MAKE FOOD LIKE CEREAL AND SYRUP

"CROPS ARE A VERY IMPORTANT PART OF FARMING. ALTHOUGH MANY TYPES OF CROPS CAN BE GROWN, THESE ARE THE SIX GROWN MOST OFTEN AND HOW THEY ARE USED."

OLLIE, HOW DO YOUR PLANTS AND GARDENS GROW?

WELL, JOHNNIE, THAT'S ACTUALLY REALLY INTERESTING!

WOW!

FIRST THE SEED IS PLANTED INTO THE GROUND

THE FARMER WATERS THE SEED TO HELP IT GROW INTO A PLANT

FARMER OLLIE EXPLAINED TO THUMBS UP JOHNNIE HOW THEIR CROPS GREW FROM A TINY SEED TO A PLANT FULL OF VEGETABLES. IT TOOK RICH DIRT, THE RIGHT AMOUNT OF WATER, THE MAGIC SCIENCE OF SUNLIGHT, AND A LOT OF LOVE AND CARE!

THE SUN SHINES AND THE PLANT TURNS THE LIGHT INTO FOOD FOR ITSELF

WITH A LOT OF CARE, TIME AND LOVE, THE PLANT WILL GROW AND PRODUCE A FRUIT OR VEGETABLE THAT CAN BE PICKED AND EATEN!

A Full Day ON THE FARM

FIRST THING
BEFORE BREAKFAST, EWELA AND BUTTON FEED THE ANIMALS AND MAKE SURE THEY ARE HEALTHY AND HAPPY

MID MORNING
ELI AND OLLIE GO OUT TO THE FIELDS TO CHECK ON THE CROPS

EARLY MORNING
AFTER BREAKFAST, EWELA AND BUTTON HEAD TO SCHOOL

LATE MORNING
OLLIE TENDS TO HER VEGETABLE GARDEN: WATER, WEEDING, AND FEEDING

EVENING
EVERYONE COMES TOGETHER
FOR DINNER AND FAMILY TIME
BEFORE GOING TO BED
AND STARTING AGAIN!

LATE AFTERNOON
THE JONES (AND FRIENDS)
TAKE SOIL SAMPLES TO
MAKE SURE THE CROPS
CAN GROW WELL

KICKFLITTER FARMS

EARLY AFTERNOON
ELI TUNES UP THE FARM
EQUIPMENT TO KEEP IT
RUNNING SMOOTHLY

THUMBS UP JOHNNIE CAME BACK LATER THAT WEEK WITH MORE OF HIS HOMEMADE HONEY AND TO SPEND THE DAY HELPING OUT AT KICKFLITTER FARMS. FROM SUNRISE TO SUNSET THERE WAS A LOT TO DO TO KEEP THE FARM FRESH. FARMER ELI TOLD JOHNNIE THAT IT WAS HARD WORK, BUT HE LOVED WATCHING HIS FARM AND FAMILY GROW.

THIS BOOK IS DEDICATED TO ALL O
AND GROW THE FOOD THAT STARTS A

"IT'S AMAZING HOW MANY THINGS COME FROM FARMS. THE JONES FAMILY GROWS THE WHEAT TO MAKE BREAD AND SO MUCH MORE!"

"THE CHEESE IS MADE OUT OF MILK FROM OUR COWS, AND THE BAKED POTATOES ARE GROWN IN THE FIELD!"

HE FARM FAMILIES WHO PLANT, SOW, LOVE, SEED AND ENDS UP ON THE TABLE!

HELP EWELA GET THROUGH THE "MAIZE" TO REACH JOHNNIE!

FILL IN THE BLANKS THEN FIND THE WORD!

TR _ CT _ R

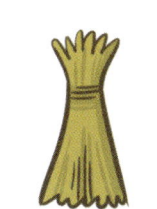

H _ Y

F _ EL _

B _ _ N

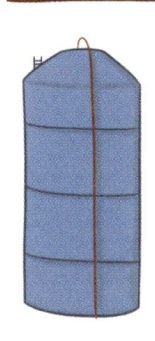

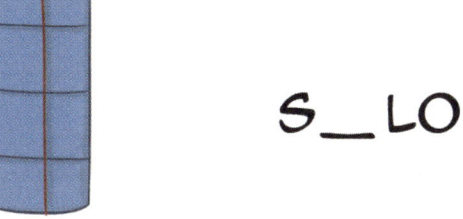

S _ LO

A X V L H A Y
V F L P T S R
B I O M W G S
A E Q S P L I
R L V M R I L
N D B B W L O
T R A C T O R
B O L V Y Q X
N P T W L R A

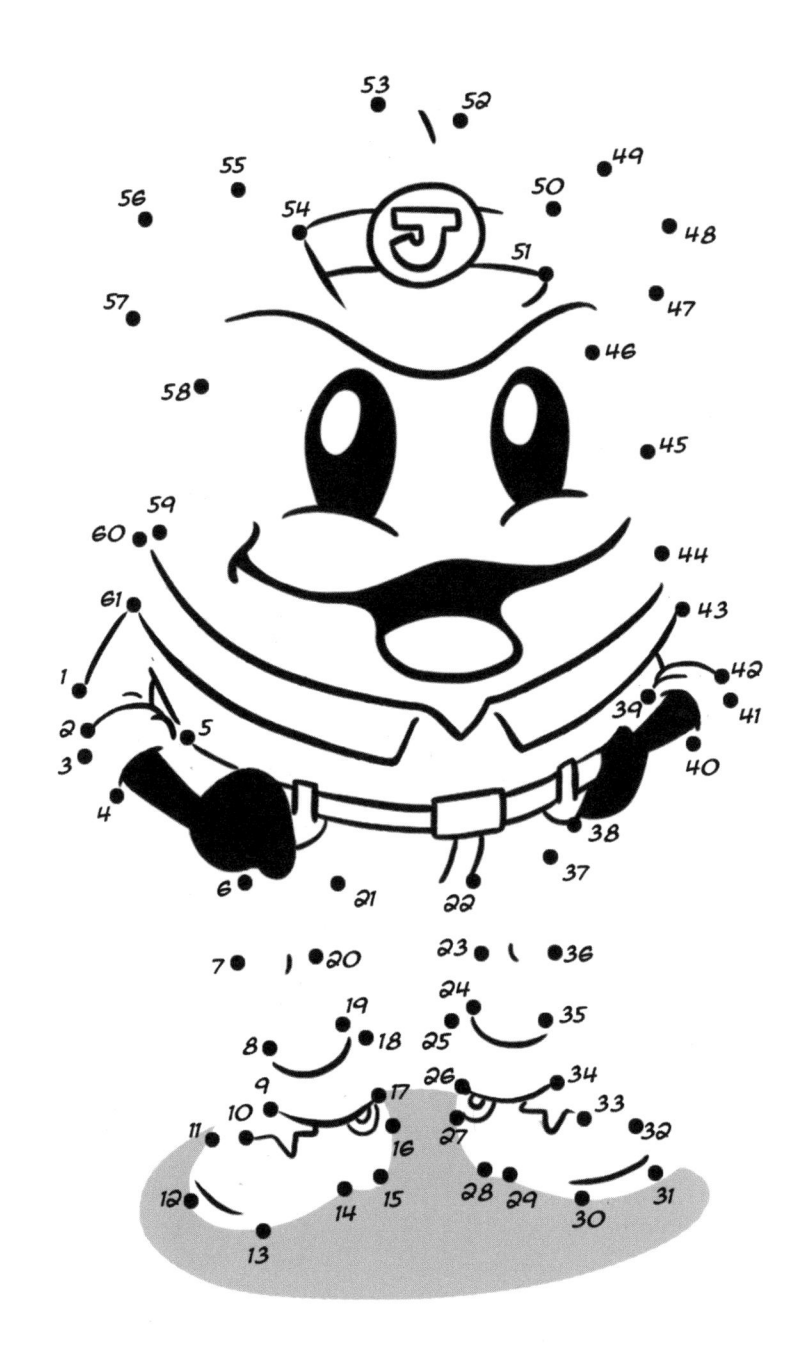

CONNECT THE DOTS AND COLOR FARMER JOHNNIE!

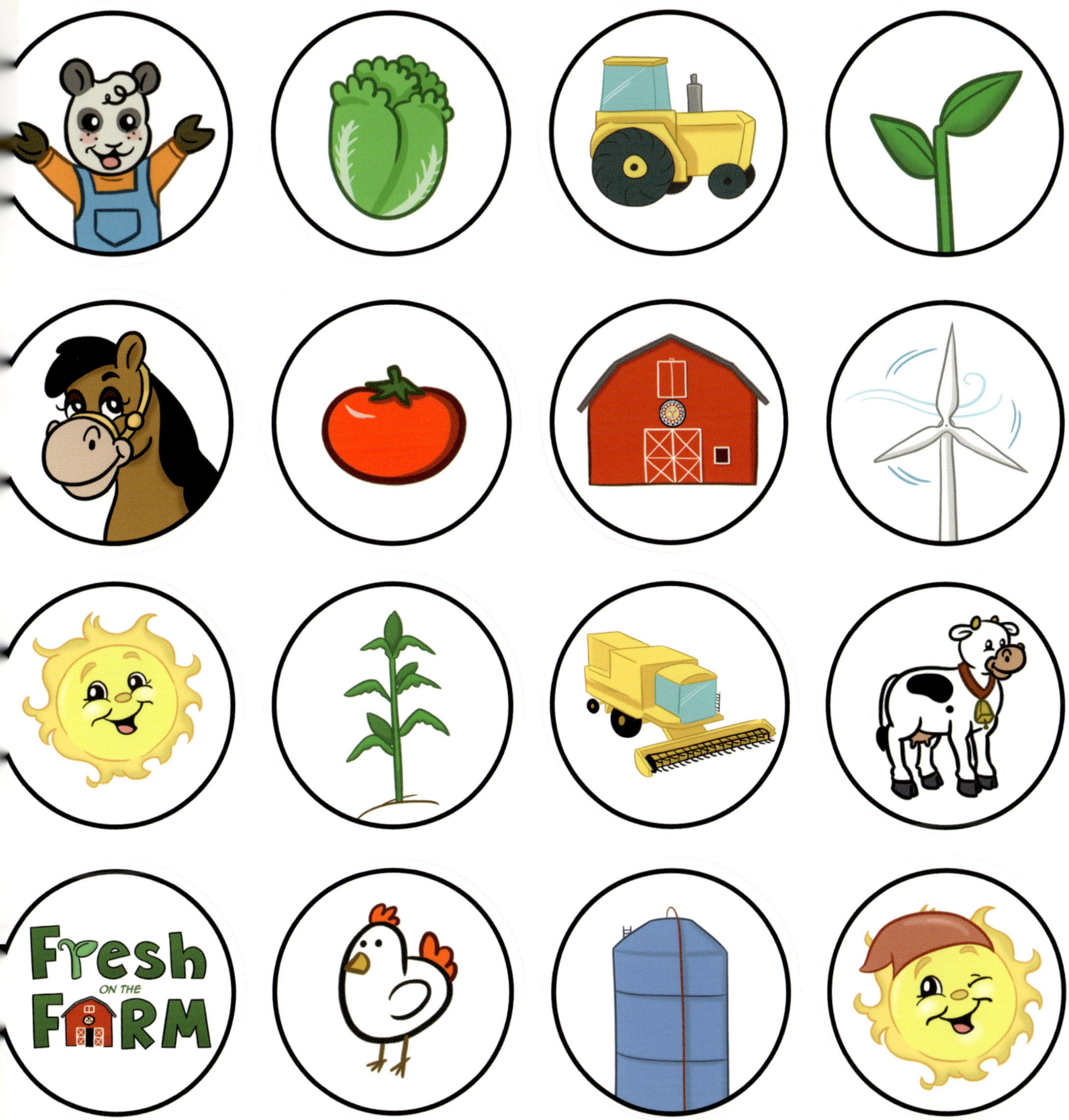
Fresh
ON THE
FARM